UNDERSTANDING
POLITICAL
SYSTEMS

WHAT IS A DEMOCRACY?

ROBYN HARDYMAN

Gareth Stevens
Publishing

Please visit our website, www.garethstevens.com. For a free color catalog of all our high-quality books, call toll free 1-800-542-2595 or fax 1-877-542-2596.

Library of Congress Cataloging-in-Publication Data

Hardyman, Robyn.
What is a democracy? / Robyn Hardyman G.
    pages cm. — (Understanding political systems)
Includes index.
ISBN 978-1-4824-0307-7 (pbk.)
ISBN 978-1-4824-0309-1 (6-pack)
ISBN 978-1-4824-0306-0 (library binding)
1. Democracy—Juvenile literature. I. Title.
JC423.H263 2014
321.8—dc23
                            2013028413

First Edition

Published in 2014 by
Gareth Stevens Publishing
111 East 14th Street, Suite 349
New York, NY 10003

© 2014 Gareth Stevens Publishing

Produced by Calcium, www.calciumcreative.co.uk
Designed by Keith Williams and Paul Myerscough
Edited by Sarah Eason

Photo credits: Cover: Shutterstock: Peeradach Rattanakoses (left), Jorg Hackemann (right). Inside: Dreamstime: Americanspirit 19, Auremar 30, Cugianza84 16, Dutourdumonde 37, Featureflash 21, Jborzicchi 38, Kcphotos 29, Kobby Dagan 45, Kuosumo 20, Maijaliisa 24, Maxcrepory 40, Mesutdogan 28, Mhanno 35, Miflippo 1, 31, Mmeeds 14, Nickolayv 8, Onepony 7, Rnonstx 15, Rorem 23, Sadikgulec 36, Shalomyoseph 4, Smandy 5, 18, Tormentor 6, Vladirochka 9, Wanghanan 41, Webphoto99 44, Welcomia 13, Wickedgood 42, Xiaofeng123 43; Shutterstock: 1000 Words 34, Arindambanerjee 32, Bloomua 33, Steven Cashmore 26, Sadik Gulec 27, Ortodox 17; Wikimedia: The British Library/Earthsound 11, Nathaniel Currier 12, Ch. Chusseau-Flaviens 25, Sir Anthony van Dyck 10, Ipankonin 22, Racoles 39.

Printed in the United States of America

CPSIA compliance information: Batch # CW14GS: For further information contact Gareth Stevens, New York, New York at 1-800-542-2595.

Contents

CHAPTER ONE

The Development of Democracy

A democracy is a form of government in which ordinary people take part in governing or running their country. The idea of democracy was first expressed in ancient Greece, and the word "democracy" comes from the Greek language. "Demos" means people, and "krates" means rule, so "democracy" means "rule by the people." In a democracy, the people decide how their community should be run. In his Gettysburg Address, US president Abraham Lincoln (1809–1865) defined democracy as, "the government of the people, by the people, for the people."

DIRECT DEMOCRACY

There are two main types of democracy. In a direct democracy, every citizen has the right to make laws and decisions together. This can work well in a small, simple community. In a whole country, it is impossible to gather everyone together to make decisions all the time. Modern societies are also complex, so the people who make the decisions require some expert knowledge. This is why direct democracies, in which all the citizens of one country vote on all decisions made, are not suitable for governing countries.

> ▼ In a democracy, the people have the right to express their views peacefully in public, even if they disagree with the government.

▲ These voters in Senegal, Africa, are voting in their presidential election.

REPRESENTATIVE DEMOCRACY

In a representative democracy, the people of a community choose, or elect, representatives to make the laws and decisions for them. At the national level, the representatives are politicians, such as members of congress. The people choose their representatives in elections every few years, in which all citizens may vote. In office, the representatives must represent the views of the people who elected them. If the people do not approve of their decisions, the representatives can be voted out of office at the next election. This ensures that, although the people of a country or state do not vote on every decision made, the final authority in the state belongs to the people.

UNDERSTANDING BETTER

A REFERENDUM

One modern-day example of direct democracy in action is a referendum. This is a vote by all the people on a particular issue. Governments may hold a referendum on an issue that is especially important for a nation's future. For example, in 2005 several countries in the European Union held a referendum on proposed changes to the European Constitution. Some critics think the people should not be given this powerful vote, because they may not fully understand the issues on which they are voting. The people may also vote for their own benefit, rather than for the good of the whole nation. What do you think?

The History of Democracy

Today, democracy is a widespread system of government around the world. Most countries have some form of democracy. Democracy is certainly not a new idea. From the earliest times, some societies tried to include at least some part of the population in deciding how their community should be run. Over many centuries, this style of government has spread across the globe.

POWERFUL RULERS

For most of history, states were ruled by a single, powerful leader. He, or sometimes she, was a king, queen, emperor, or even a dictator. The ruler seized power, inherited it, or gained it because they were part of an elite group, such as a landowner or a military leader. However, these rulers could not govern entirely alone. They often set up institutions to help them rule, and these institutions could represent the interests of at least some of the people. Sometimes, these institutions grew in power, especially if the ruler needed their support. They gradually increased their control over the ruler's behavior. Over time, in some cases, these institutions came to represent more and more of the people. They gained enough power to share the running of the country with the ruler, and for their countries to become more democratic.

This is a winged statue of Democracy. It stands in front of Union Station in Washington, D.C.

UNDERSTANDING BETTER

CELEBRATING DEMOCRACY

In 2008, Canada celebrated 250 years of democracy. The country's first elected assembly met on October 2, 1758. Yet, in a poll conducted in 2013, only 55 percent of people said they were satisfied with the democracy in their country, 20 percent fewer than 10 years before. Many factors have contributed to this lack of satisfaction, but the poll shows that democracy is an ever-changing form of government. Can you think of ways that democracies have to change to suit the times they are in?

In 2008, Canadians celebrated the fact that their country had been a parliamentary democracy for 250 years. As part of the campaign, people worked on ways to engage more young Canadians in the democratic process.

WHO ARE THE PEOPLE?

The idea of who "the people" are has changed a great deal over time. Early democracies would not seem very democratic to us today, as the definition of a "citizen" was limited to a small part of the male population. Women were excluded from politics for many years and have only in recent history been given the vote. However, over the centuries, the right to vote was extended to more groups in society. Today, a true democracy includes all walks of life—whatever a person's gender, religion, race, or status.

Democracy in the Ancient World

Democracy appeared for the first time thousands of years ago, in ancient Greece. At that time, the country consisted of a group of city-states. Each was independent, with a strong capital city. Some of the best-known city-states were Athens, Sparta, Thebes, and Corinth. The strongest was Athens, which is now considered to be the birthplace of democracy.

ATHENS

The city-state of Athens was the home of the first democracy, in the fifth century BC. It was a direct democracy. Its citizens met together in the assembly to vote on laws and other issues, such as going to war. They also elected their own leader. Men who had completed two years of military service were citizens, whatever their wealth. Women were excluded, however, and so were foreigners and slaves.

Everyday matters were decided by the Council of Five Hundred, whose members were all men who had been chosen by lot. This was a system of randomly choosing people to prevent individuals from gaining control of the Council.

In this painting of ancient Greek philosophers, Plato and Aristotle are standing in the center. Plato is on the left, with Aristotle on the right. It was painted by the Italian artist Raphael between 1509 and 1511.

Pericles was the leader of Athens from about 460 to 429 BC, when the city-state was at its height. He was a strong supporter of democracy. He restricted the powers of the unelected council and brought reforms to the legal system.

UNDERSTANDING BETTER

CRITICS OF DEMOCRACY

Two of the greatest philosophers of ancient Greece were not in favor of democracy. Plato (c.427–347 BC) thought that governing should only be carried out by men with the right training and skills. Aristotle (384–322 BC) thought that democracy was an unstable system because powerful individuals could influence the assembly and make them vote unwisely. He believed government should be run by the wealthy, who do not need to work and have time for political duties. This is very different from what we think today about giving everyone access to political office. What do you think?

ANCIENT ROME

For centuries, ancient Rome in Italy was governed as a republic. It was not a democracy, but it had some democratic elements. The two leaders, the consuls, were elected every year. Their power was controlled by the senate, a group of wealthy citizens who ruled for life. All citizens could serve in the assembly, which voted on certain laws and issues of war and peace. In 45 BC, the military leader Julius Caesar took hold of power for himself and ancient Rome became an empire that dominated much of the world. For the next 400 years the Roman Empire was ruled by an emperor. Democracy would not reappear for many centuries.

Medieval and Early Modern Europe

After the end of the Roman Empire, Europe split into a collection of small nations, ruled by powerful individuals. For 600 years, society was strictly hierarchical. The king was at the top, with the churchmen, lords, and landowners in the middle, and the peasant farmers at the bottom. Very few people had any say in how their country was governed.

INSTITUTIONS OF DEMOCRACY

Some of the institutions of democracy did begin to develop during medieval times, however. In the 900s, in Iceland, an assembly of chiefs called the Althing met to vote on laws and settle arguments. This has been called the first parliament in Europe. In other countries, the king would gather a council of the most powerful lords to advise him and approve the taxes he wanted to raise. Over time, these assemblies came to represent not just the nobility but also the clergy, and the people. These groups became known as the Three Estates, and they could voice their grievances at an assembly.

In the 1640s, the English parliament briefly triumphed over the king in the English Civil War, and King Charles I was executed. The monarchy was restored in 1660.

King John signed the Magna Carta in 1215, but he was soon in conflict with his barons again. The charter was reissued many times and accepted by later kings. It became a key document of the English constitution.

PARLIAMENT

In England from the 1200s, the representative assembly was called parliament. Parliament grew in power over the centuries and became the source of new laws. Although England saw a shift in power in which people gained more control, this change did not happen all over Europe. In many European countries, monarchs ruled with more absolute power and democracy stalled. In 1689, the English parliament forced the king to sign the Declaration of Rights. This established the democratic principles of free, fair, and frequent elections, and freedom of speech in parliament.

UNDERSTANDING BETTER

MAGNA CARTA: A WRITTEN CONSTITUTION?

The Magna Carta (meaning Great Charter) is one of the founding documents of democracy. In 1215, the barons forced King John of England to sign it. He had ruled unwisely and spent too much money on wars. The document limited his power by stating that he could not raise taxes without the barons' permission, or imprison people at will. The principle that the law must be freely available to all was important in the development of democracy. How do you think the Magna Carta changed the lives of ordinary citizens?

The American Revolution

In the eighteenth century, the British tradition of parliament extended to the thirteen colonies in North America. These communities had their own assemblies, and some control over their government. Before long, they began to resent Britain's demand for taxes. They thought these payments to a faraway country were unfair. Life in North America was about to change.

"NO TAXATION WITHOUT REPRESENTATION!"

The colonists complained about paying taxes to Britain when they had no representation in the British parliament. In 1775, a series of rebellions started in North America that became known as the American Revolution. Britain responded by sending more troops across the Atlantic to try to restore law and order. However, in the decade that followed, Britain began to lose its grip on government in North America. Finally, in 1783, the British were defeated. A new constitution was drafted for the United States of America.

In 1773 in Boston, colonists complained about taxes from Britain, and the East India Company, which controlled the import of tea to America. When officials refused to return three shiploads of taxed tea to Britain, some colonists boarded the ships and threw the tea into Boston Harbor. The incident was later called The Boston Tea Party.

> Thomas Jefferson was one of the most important of presidents. His face is famously carved into rock at Mount Rushmore, South Dakota.

A FEDERAL STRUCTURE

The newly founded United States of America was a nation made up of a federation of states. Each state retained its own government and laws, serving the particular needs of its citizens. The federal (national) government made laws of national importance. The new constitution was based on democratic principles, and ensured that no branch of the federal government could become too powerful. It was the beginning of a new system of government for North America and the founding of what is still the world's most powerful democratic nation.

UNDERSTANDING BETTER

THE DECLARATION OF INDEPENDENCE

In 1776, one of the leaders of the colonists, Thomas Jefferson, wrote the Declaration of Independence. In it he wrote: "We hold these truths to be self-evident, that all men are created equal, that they are endowed by their Creator with certain unalienable Rights, that among these are Life, Liberty, and the pursuit of Happiness." Government, he says, exists for the good of the people, and takes its power from the people. What do you think Jefferson is saying about the rights of the individual? What is the meaning of "unalienable?" How did this relate to the colonists' experience of British rule?

The Nineteenth Century

During the 1700s in Britain, the authority of parliament grew. The monarch needed its support to govern. Members of parliament divided loosely into political parties, and the idea of a chief minister supported by the biggest party, the prime minister, evolved. Over the next 200 years, almost all western European countries, as well as the United States, Canada, Australia, and New Zealand, developed democratic systems.

REVOLUTION AND CIVIL WAR

One important influence on this was the French Revolution. In the late 1700s, radicals in France overthrew the monarch and passed a Declaration of Rights that stated that "The source of all sovereignty resides essentially in the nation." After centuries of rule by kings, the ordinary people of France began to take power and the governance of their country into their own hands. In Britain too, a series of Reform Acts in the 1800s extended the franchise, or right to vote, to many more people. Both Germany and France gave all men the voting rights.

The French people still celebrate Bastille Day on July 14 each year. This was the date in 1789 on which the revolutionaries stormed the Bastille, a large prison in the center of Paris.

SLAVERY

In the United States, all adult white men had the right to vote by the mid-1800s. However, the existence of slavery in the southern states was a blot on this democratic progress. The North called for its abolition, and the Civil War that followed in 1861–1865 resulted in the defeat of the South, the abolition of slavery, and the extension of the franchise to African American men. It would take another century, however, for African Americans to achieve complete political equality.

▼ African American slaves were forced to work on plantations in southern states. They lived in cabins such as these at Boone Hall Plantation and Gardens in Mount Pleasant, South Carolina.

UNDERSTANDING BETTER

THE INDUSTRIAL REVOLUTION

Another, more peaceful revolution affected the development of democracy. The Industrial Revolution, which began in Britain, brought great technological developments and changed societies forever. It created a wealthy middle class of industrialists, and the working class moved from the land to the factories and cities. Why do you think this affected the move toward democracy? Why did these people think they had the right to vote for their elected representatives in government?

The Twentieth Century

During the twentieth century, democracy faced many challenges from more absolute, authoritarian forms of government. However, by the end of the century, democracy was still the dominant form of government in many parts of world. The steady progress of democracy, spanning hundreds of years, made this type of government widely accepted throughout the world.

SOCIALISM

After the great turmoil of World War I (1914–1918), many states became more committed to democracy. Ordinary men and women could vote, and political parties grew to represent their interests. Socialists, for example, argued for a more equal distribution of wealth in society, to give a better standard of living to the poor. They thought that political equality was of little use to them unless they had more economic equality, too.

FASCISM

One political system that posed a threat to democracy, however, was fascism. This system favored strong, centralized government and banned all forms of opposition. Fascist governments took control in Germany, Italy, and Spain in the 1920s and 1930s and facism became a powerful political force. When Germany's fascist leader, Adolf Hitler, invaded neighboring countries, his actions led to World War II (1939–1945), one of the most devastating wars the world has ever seen. However, the defeat of Germany and Italy in that conflict brought an end to fascist rule in both countries.

Hitler was the leader of an extreme right-wing political party called the Nazi Party. The swastika symbol was used on the Nazi Party's flag and has since become associated with the Nazi movement.

ANTIFASCISM

During the conflict of World War II, the US government produced propaganda to persuade people to support the war effort. It included posters such as one that showed a "two-headed monster of the Germans and the Japanese," and urged people to work hard in factories to produce goods that were needed for the war. What messages do you think such posters were intended to give?

COMMUNISM

Another challenge to democracy came from a political system called communism, in the Soviet Union and elsewhere. In this extreme form of socialism, the state controlled all wealth, to give a better standard of living to the poorest people. However, to achieve these goals, a single party governed with absolute authority. As a result, the people had no say, and most continued to live in poverty. When communism began to fail, the Soviet Union broke up in 1991, and democracy gradually emerged in the Soviet Union's former member countries.

Lenin was the first leader of the Communist government that took over in Russia after a revolution in 1917. The old Russian Empire became the Soviet Union. Lenin's rule was undemocratic. The Communist Party had total control. Lenin ruled until his death in 1924.

CHAPTER TWO

How Democracy Works

Democracies vary in detail around the world, but all are representative democracies at the national level. Elected representatives create and vote on laws, and make decisions about how a country should be run. However, the basis of their power lies with ordinary people. The representatives can be voted out of office at the next election if the people do not approve of their policies.

THE CONSTITUTION

A constitution is a set of rules and principles that lays out how a nation should be governed. This fundamental document places limits on the power of government, and guarantees the political rights and freedom of individuals, even against the majority. Most countries, such as the United States, have a written constitution. It has been added to, or amended, many times since it was first written in 1787. The United Kingdom, on the other hand, does not. Its "unwritten constitution" is determined by its historical customs, laws, and habits.

During Zambia's recent general elections, people lined up for hours to be able to cast their vote to elect a president and representatives to the country's National Assembly.

In many democratic elections, voters mark their preferred candidate on the ballot paper and put it in the ballot box. Their vote is anonymous so their choice remains secret.

THREE BRANCHES OF GOVERNMENT

There are three branches of government in a democracy. The ways in which they work together vary in different countries. They generally are: the executive branch, which creates policies and carries them out; the legislature, which debates and approves the laws proposed by the executive branch; and the judiciary, or the courts and judges. The judiciary decides whether laws have been broken, and settles arguments about interpretations of the law. The principle of the Separation of Powers ensures that these three branches of government remain independent of each other, to prevent any one of them becoming too powerful.

UNDERSTANDING BETTER

A GOOD SYSTEM?

Critics of democracy suggest that giving power to all the people can lead to bad government. English playwright George Bernard Shaw said, "Democracy substitutes election by the incompetent many for appointment by the corrupt few." US president Franklin D. Roosevelt (1882–1945) said, "Democracy cannot succeed unless those who express their choice are prepared to choose wisely. The real safeguard of democracy, therefore, is education." And British Prime Minister Winston Churchill (1874–1965) said, "The best argument against democracy is a five-minute conversation with the average voter." What do you think about giving a say to everyone, regardless of their social status or education?

The Executive Branch

In a democracy, the executive branch is responsible for the day-to-day running of the country. It makes policy and puts it into action. It is sometimes called "the government." This part of a political system is most closely linked to ordinary people. It tries to keep up with public opinion, while also working to create policies that are affordable, achievable, and in the best interests of the people they govern.

ELECTED MEMBERS

The members of the executive branch are secretaries or elected politicians. They are often called ministers, and each one has responsibility for a particular area of government, such as health, education, or foreign affairs. In the United States, the minister responsible for foreign affairs is called the Secretary of State, while in Britain he or she is called the Foreign Secretary. Members of the executive branch meet together as a group, in cabinet, to discuss their decisions and make policy. The members of the executive branch do not make the laws, but they do put forward ideas about how laws could be created or changed.

CHIEF EXECUTIVE

The executive branch is led by the chief executive. This person has different names in different countries. In the United States he or she is the

This is the US Department of the Treasury, in Washington D.C. The treasury forms part of the federal government. It was established by an Act of Congress in 1789, to manage government revenue. The Secretary of the treasury, who runs it, is a member of the executive branch of the government.

US presidents, such as Barack Obama, often pay visits to British prime ministers, such as David Cameron. Heads of government frequently pay visits to each other's countries, to maintain good relations between the countries.

president. Britain has a prime minister as its chief executive and Germany has a chancellor. Chancellor Angela Merkel was the first woman ever to hold this office in Germany. She leads a coalition of several political parties in the country's government. She is a powerful figure within the European Union, too. In a presidential system, the chief executive is also the Head of State. In Britain, the monarch is the Head of State, and the prime minister is the leader of the largest political party in the legislature, or parliament.

UNDERSTANDING BETTER

PUTTING POLICY INTO PRACTICE

The government employs a large group of people to put their policies into effect. These people are not elected, they are professionals in the public administration. They develop expertise in their chosen area of policy during their careers, and work out the details of how any changes will happen. Do you think these public servants, or civil servants, have power in a democracy? Can you think how they could influence the extent to which new policies actually come into effect? Is this democratic?

The Legislature and the Judiciary

The legislature makes laws. The way it works is defined in the constitution, but it is made up of elected representatives of the people. It is often called a parliament, assembly, or congress. The legislature acts as a check on the executive branch, by debating its proposals and deciding which should become law. The judiciary is the system of courts and judges that carries out justice. It interprets laws made by the legislature, and acts to protect the rights of citizens.

DIFFERENT SYSTEMS

In the United States, the legislative assembly and the executive branch are separate. The president is not a member, but is elected in a separate presidential election. In a parliamentary system, such as in the United Kingdom, Germany, and India, there is one election for both bodies. The executive branch members sit in the legislature, and are drawn from the political party with the most seats in the assembly. The legislature often consists of two assemblies. In the US, congress consists of the House of Representatives and the Senate. Both are elected. In the United Kingdom, parliament is the House of Commons and the House of Lords. The lords are appointed, not elected. The second chamber acts as a brake to hold back any hasty decisions from the first.

This is the seal of the United States congress. In Congress, the House of Representatives has 435 members and the Senate has 100, two from each state.

THE JURY SYSTEM

One feature of the judicial system in a democracy is "trial by jury." When certain cases come to court, the outcome is decided by a jury of ordinary citizens, chosen at random from the population. They hear the arguments for and against in a case, and decide if the person is guilty or innocent. Usually, everyone on the jury must decide the same way for a decision to be valid. This is called a unanimous decision. Do you think this is a fair or effective system? Can the jurors be impartial, or neutral in their thinking? Can they understand the issues?

This is the US Supreme Court, in Washington D.C. It is the highest court in the land. It consists of a chief justice and eight associate justices. They are nominated by the president and are confirmed by the Senate. The justices keep their seats for life.

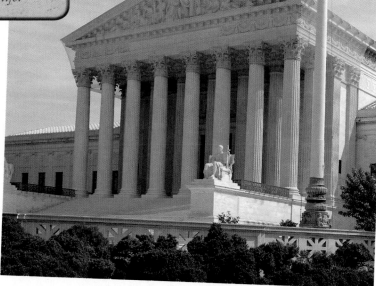

A CONTROLLING INFLUENCE

The judiciary consists of a system of courts, starting with smaller, local ones, and ending with a supreme court. This is the ultimate decision maker and the court of final appeal. State courts try most of the cases that come to law. However, extreme or controversial cases are often taken to the supreme court for special attention.

Political Parties and Elections

Democracies represent the will of the people. However, people have different views on how they want their country to be run. Their representatives therefore organize themselves into rival groups, or political parties. In a democracy, people choose which party to support. The way to decide which party has the most control over decision making is to hold elections.

PARTIES AND ELECTIONS

Political parties set out the choice for voters in elections. Some parties, such as the US Democratic Party, represent a wide range of views on many issues. Others, such as the Green Party, are more focused in their objectives. The party that has the most representatives elected to the legislature is in control of policy making, until the next election. In some countries, such as Germany, many parties win seats and they form a coalition to govern. In others, such as the United States, there are only two main parties and one wins a clear majority. This produces stronger, more stable government, but the minority views have less influence.

▼ During an election campaign, some people put up signs to show which party or candidate they support. These three signs in a front yard in Arizona are all in support of the Republican party. The sign behind them is in support of a Democrat.

VOTES FOR WOMEN

The right to vote in elections is called suffrage. During the nineteenth century, the vote was gradually extended to more groups in society. Women were one of the last groups to win this right. They achieved suffrage first in New Zealand in 1893. The United States followed in 1920 and Britain in 1928. Women campaigned hard for this right, and some were injured or even killed during protests.

The women who fought for the right to vote were called suffragettes. This suffragette is campaigning on a British street in the early years of the twentieth century. Some protested peacefully, while others used more violent methods and were sent to prison.

UNDERSTANDING BETTER

EXTREME CAMPAIGNERS

The cover of a magazine for suffrage supporters in Britain showed one protester, Emily Davison, who died in a protest in 1913. She was killed when she threw herself under the king's horse at a race called the Derby in protest of the government's failure to give women the right to vote. Emily had used violence in her previous campaigns, and had been to prison. However, on the cover of the magazine she was portrayed as an angel, who "died for women." Why do you think a violent campaigner was portrayed like this?

CHAPTER THREE

Living in a Democracy

In today's world, nearly all the most powerful states are multiparty democracies. In most of the monarchies around the world, real power rests not with the monarch but with the three branches of government. There remain, however, some dictatorships, in which one leader exercises absolute power and imposes great restraints on people's freedom. The pressure for these countries to move toward democracy is increasing.

THE RESPONSIBILITIES OF GOVERNMENT

In a democracy, the people elect the government to fulfill basic functions. These include defending the country from harm or invasion, providing effective services such as health, education, roads, and utilities (such as water, gas, and electricity), and providing a support system for those most in need in society. People put their faith in elected politicians, and expect them to fulfill the promises they made when they were voted into office. This faith keeps a democracy working smoothly, without people feeling the need to protest or cause a rebellion.

People who live in a democracy have the right to peaceful protest. The Live8 concerts were peaceful protests that took place to highlight the issue of global poverty.

UNDERSTANDING BETTER

REGULAR ELECTIONS

In a democracy, people are elected to hold office in government for a limited time only. This is a good thing in one way, because it prevents the total control of power by any one party. However, it can also mean that governments make policy for the short term, in order to get re-elected. They may focus on winning the next election, rather than working for the long-term interests of the country. Terms of office often run for a number of years. Do you think this is a good or bad thing?

PLAYING A PART

In return for good government, the people have responsibilities, too. They must behave responsibly toward others to create a safe and happy society, they must obey the law, and they must try to be informed when they use their vote. A democracy only works effectively if the people in it understand the political choices presented to them, and use their vote wisely to elect a good representative government. Politicians keep a democracy running on a day-to-day basis, but the people need to play an active role, too.

This woman is voting in a recent referendum in Turkey. The referendum was a vote on important amendments to the country's constitution.

The Rule of Law

The principle of the rule of law is fundamental to the system of democracy. It means that everyone should know the law, and that the law should apply to everyone equally. Everyone, whatever their gender, race, religion, or status, must act within the law and the constitution. A government must uphold the law, to encourage law-abiding citizens and to provide a safe and stable community for everyone to live in.

STRONG INSTITUTIONS

For the rule of law to work, a country must have strong institutions. Everyone must know that the judiciary is well organized, well trained, and impartial, or without bias. They must know that public officials and institutions, at all levels in society, even the highest, can be challenged if they appear to be acting outside the law. Citizens will feel safe if they know that all arguments will be settled peacefully, and that effective action and punishment is available if they suffer harm from someone who acts against the law. If people know the law works, they are much more likely to obey it.

This statue is called "Authority of Law." It is one of a pair of statues on the steps of the US Supreme Court Building in Washington, D.C. The male figure holds a tablet of laws and the sword of justice. The female statue in the pair is called "Contemplation of Justice."

In the early twentieth century, many courtrooms looked like this one. Today, they mostly look more modern. In all courtrooms, however, the judge sits above the rest of the people during a trial. The people in the jury sit together to one side.

UNITED NATIONS

The rule of law also exists to protect people from a government that tries to abuse the powers it has been given. One of the roles of the United Nations is to protect the principle of the rule of law around the world. The United Nations is an international organization with 193 member countries. It was founded in 1945, after World War II, to promote world peace, and improve living conditions and human rights for people everywhere. It works to develop an international standard for the rule of law in many countries, especially those either experiencing wars or having recently ended them. This can be an important step on the road to creating or improving democracy in those countries.

UNDERSTANDING BETTER

JUSTICE AND INJUSTICE

"Man's capacity for justice makes democracy possible, but man's inclination to injustice makes democracy necessary." This was said by Reinhold Niebuhr in 1944. He was a religious and political thinker. What do you think the two parts of his statement mean?

Equality of Opportunity and Treatment

Another fundamental principle of democracy is that all adults have the same political rights, regardless of their gender, age, race, or religious belief. In a democracy, all people should be treated equally, whatever their situation. All citizens have a right to a safe and free life. Even those who cannot vote, such as children, are protected by the rule of law.

RACIAL EQUALITY

In the United States, democracy was denied to African American people in the South until the 1960s. Although the Constitution upheld the right of all people to vote, African Americans were denied suffrage in some states and forced to live separately, as second-class citizens. The civil rights movement, led by Martin Luther King Jr. (1929–1968), grew in protest of this. Federal laws were finally passed to ensure there was political equality throughout the country. In South Africa, a similar situation existed. The white minority dominated the country, and nonwhite South Africans had few rights. The first multiracial election in South Africa, based on universal suffrage, finally took place in 1994.

In a modern democracy, all people should have the right to be treated equally. In the workplace, everyone should have the same opportunities, regardless of their gender or status.

GENDER EQUALITY

We have seen that women had to fight harder than men to gain the right to vote in national elections. Since then, many democracies have passed legislation that also protects the rights of men and women to equal opportunity and treatment, in the workplace and elsewhere. Laws also protect against discrimination on the grounds of age and religious belief. Children are also protected by laws. Although the voting age is 18 in many democracies, adults there have passed laws on behalf of children to ensure their safety.

This is the first page of the original Constitution of the United States, written in 1787. It is the highest law in the land. It outlines the principles of the government, and how the people will be provided with justice, civil peace, defense, and freedom.

UNDERSTANDING BETTER

HUMAN RIGHTS

In 1948, the United Nations adopted the Universal Declaration of Human Rights. This document lays out the basic rights that all humans should have, anywhere in the world. Humans are free, and entitled to rights without gender, race, religious, or wealth discrimination. Their rights include: equal treatment under the law, privacy at home, freedom to travel, to own property, to take part in government, to work, to education, to adequate living standards, and to express an opinion. These rights underpin all democracies. Why do you think the document was drawn up shortly after the end of World War II?

Freedom of Speech

The freedom to express an opinion, and to seek and receive information, is another important principle of democracy. People can say what they think of the government without fear of being arrested, as long as they break no laws. In a democracy, it is usually against the law to encourage hatred or violence in other people, on grounds of religion or other factors.

THE MEDIA

The government must know what people think and want, in order to be able to respond to their needs. Individuals can speak out alone, but in complex societies the media has the most powerful voice in expressing different opinions. Newspapers, broadcasters, and Internet media are powerful forces in a democracy.

They can investigate and expose wrongdoing in government. For example, British newspapers exposed the recent scandal of members of parliament making dishonest financial claims for their expenses. In 1972, American journalists exposed the wrongdoing of President Nixon in the Watergate scandal, forcing him to resign.

This woman is taking part in an anticapitalist march in Canada. She has the right in a democracy to express her point of view peacefully, without fear of being attacked.

There are many ways to access the media today. Newspapers are still printed, but many people also read them online. News sources are available 24 hours a day and we have to consider whether we think a source is biased in favor of one point of view.

POWERFUL INFLUENCE

The media can also influence public opinion. Coverage of all news stories can be biased, but in important events, such as a decision to go to war, or in a general election, a journalist should be impartial because people can be influenced by the opinions they read or hear. Media reports have the power to reinforce someone's own beliefs, or to persuade them to make a particular judgment.

UNDERSTANDING BETTER

PROFIT FIRST?

Newspapers and other media forms are commercial businesses. Along with wanting to tell the truth and encourage debate, they need to sell newspapers, or attract the most viewers, to make a profit. Some people say this has made them trivialize or simplify the issues, and concentrate more on the personalities of people in public life, rather than their policies. They have been invading people's privacy to get at a "sensational" story. What do you think? Has the media lost its way as an effective check on government?

CHAPTER FOUR

Fighting for Democracy

Many countries around the world are engaged in a struggle to achieve a more democratic government. For some of these countries, decades of dictatorships have left the people powerless, and fighting for democracy is a challenging task. Other countries are facing serious poverty. When day-to-day life is a struggle for food, water, and shelter, it's very difficult for people to find the energy to take part in political decisions.

AFRICA

In the second half of the twentieth century, the countries of Africa that had been colonies of European countries gained their independence. Although parliamentary regimes were often set up, few survived. Powerful individuals established dictatorships, or the military seized control. Civil wars followed in many countries. Stable, democratic government is still not widespread in Africa, mainly because there is so much poverty. People's main concerns are for food, shelter, and work, rather than political freedom. Many receive little education. In 2002, the African Union was formed. All African countries are members except Morocco. They have committed to help improve the continent's democracy, human rights, and economy, by bringing an end to conflicts and promoting cooperation.

In Thailand, southeast Asia, supporters of the deposed prime minister, Thaksin Shinawatra, recently took to the streets. They were commemorating their dead and wounded from a few months earlier, when the army cracked down on them. Democracy is still fragile in Thailand.

THE ARAB SPRING

In late 2010 and 2011, in North Africa and the Middle East, a series of protests began against the undemocratic governments of several countries. Together they are known as "The Arab Spring." They began in Tunisia, and spread to Libya, Jordan, Egypt, Syria, and elsewhere. The governments of Tunisia, Libya, Yemen, and Egypt fell. Democratic elections have been held for the first time in decades, and the people of these countries are at last trying to determine their own future.

After revolution, Egyptians have continued to protest against their country's lack of speed in moving toward democracy.

UNDERSTANDING BETTER

SYRIA

In Syria, the protests that began with the Arab Spring have still not been resolved, and the country has collapsed into a terrible civil war. The authoritarian government led by President Bashar al-Assad has attacked the protesters with brutal force, and more than 70,000 civilians have been killed. Western countries have been reluctant to intervene with military force to stop this bloodshed. Do you think they should intervene, or should the region sort out its own problems?

Iraq and Libya

The countries of Iraq and Libya were both ruled by oppressive dictators in the late twentieth century. However, the power of democracy and lasting political change is starting to revolutionize the lives of citizens in these nations. In the early 21st century, both countries have seen their dictators overthrown, and have begun to make some progress toward a democratic style of government.

IRAQ

In Iraq, Saddam Hussein became president in 1979. His brutal, dictatorial rule continued until 2003, when a US-led coalition invaded the country and Hussein was removed from power. Democracy did not immediately follow, however. For years, different groups have been competing for power. Elections were held in 2005 and 2010, and a new constitution was drafted, but religious differences continue to cause great instability and violence in the country. Although the seeds of democracy have been sown, the future of government in this country remains uncertain.

These men campaigned in Kurdistan, Iraq, in the lead-up to the country's elections in 2010. After the election, Nouri al-Maliki, a former rebel who led the first full-time government after the toppling of Saddam Hussein, was picked for a second term as prime minister.

UNDERSTANDING BETTER

GOVERNMENT IN IRAQ

It is uncertain whether democracy can be successfully established in a country with little tradition of this form of government. Iraq contains people from many different ethnic and religious backgrounds, including the Kurds and the two branches of Islam, the Sunnis and the Shiites. Islam has become a political force, and the country may end up being ruled by religious leaders. Do you think western nations should try to encourage democracy there, or should they leave the Iraqis to find their own way?

LIBYA

Libya was ruled for more than 40 years by the dictator Colonel Muammar Gaddafi. His rule left the people powerless, any form of opposition was banned, and the dictatorship was accused of abusing human rights and of supporting terrorism. In 2011, a popular uprising against this oppressive rule finally succeeded. The United Nations supported NATO air strikes to protect civilians from the Libyan military, and Gaddafi was eventually killed. In July 2012, the election of a General National Congress was the country's first free national election in six decades.

Newspapers around the world reported the defeat and death of Colonel Gaddafi in Libya. The country's new government is preparing the ground for a constitution and, in time, full transition to democracy.

Burma

The struggle for democracy has been going on for decades in Burma, in Asia. From the early 1960s to 2011, the country was run by a brutal regime, led by military generals. They suppressed all opposition to their rule and governed with absolute power. However, one woman has been at the forefront of Burma's campaign for a more democratic future. There are now signs that change may be on the way.

AUNG SAN SUU KYI

In the early 1960s, Burma's new leader, Aung San, was assassinated. His daughter Aung San Suu Kyi lived in Britain for many years, but when she returned to Burma in 1988 she decided to stay to help the people in their struggle for democracy. Although she was placed under house arrest for almost 15 years, she still led the National League for Democracy (NLD). Finally, the military rulers agreed to democratic elections in 1991, which the NLD won. However, it was a hollow victory. Aung San Suu Kyi should have become prime minister, but the military refused and instead she and her party were still persecuted.

Aung San Suu Kyi has been a powerful international symbol of peaceful resistance to oppression and a campaigner for democracy.

UNDERSTANDING BETTER

STEPS FORWARD

In August 2012, the government of Burma announced that it would stop censoring the media. Many political prisoners were also released. In November 2012, President Obama visited the country. This was a clear signal that Burma was emerging from its long political isolation. President Obama spoke of the importance of four freedoms: to speak, to associate, to worship, and to live without fear, and he said that in a democracy the most important "office holder" was "the citizen." Can you think how this recognition from the outside world might affect the Burmese people's struggle for democracy?

In January 2013, the Burmese government finally abolished the 25-year-old ban on public gatherings of more than five people.

HOPE FOR THE FUTURE

Since 2010, the situation in Burma has improved. In 2012, the NLD won many seats in by-elections for parliament, the results were accepted, and Aung San Suu Kyi finally took her seat. It was a momentous occasion for this political leader who had struggled for years to make her voice heard. Now the challenge remains to keep up this momentum for change, and for the NLD to be allowed to govern if it wins the general election in 2015.

CHAPTER FIVE

The Future for Democracy

Today, all the world's most powerful states have democratic governments, apart from China. Many other countries are striving for it. However, democracy, though popular, also faces great challenges. In some established democracies, governments are struggling to keep their citizens involved in the political process. Others are facing the challenge of upholding people's freedom against the rule of law.

LOSING INTEREST?

In western countries that have enjoyed democracy for a long time, people have become less interested in politics and play a less active part in their democracy. Many people never vote in elections. They have less trust in the will of their politicians to represent their views, and think they have little or no chance of influencing policy. Political parties in the United States and Europe are funded by big business or wealthy individuals who, in turn, may influence policy and pay for lavish election campaigns. It would be dangerous, however, to take our democracy for granted.

In many wealthy countries such as the United States, people are becoming less interested in politics. Only about half the population votes in US presidential elections.

North Korea is one of the most undemocratic countries in the world. This statue is of Kim Il-Sung, leader of the ruling Communist Party for much of the twentieth century. He is known as the country's "eternal president," although he died in 1994.

NEW DEMOCRACIES

There is a growing international recognition of the importance of human rights, and that these rights are best preserved in a democracy. For the newly developing economies of the world to establish successful democracies, they need to ensure three things. First, that there are honest and committed individuals to hold office in government; second, that enough people are educated to serve in the public administration; and, third, that the judiciary, the media, and other institutions can act as powerful, independent checks on the government.

UNDERSTANDING BETTER

THE CHALLENGE OF TERRORISM

The problem of terrorism poses a challenge to democracies today. How should governments deal with this threat and still maintain the rule of law and human rights? Terrorists use violence against innocent people to promote their political ideas. If there is clear evidence against them, they can be tried using the law. But what about people suspected of plotting terrorist acts? Should they be imprisoned without trial, to prevent them from acting? This may be a breach of their liberty, but is it justifiable because of the greater threat to the safety of the population? What do you think?

China

China is the world's second largest economy, but it remains a communist country. In 1989, a protest movement for democracy was violently suppressed by the government. The Communist Party has absolute power and still cracks down on any opposition. In a world where most countries give citizens a voice, can or will this economic superpower move to a more democratic government?

MANY PROBLEMS

A democratic future for China does not look likely. Despite its economic success, the country faces many problems. Millions of people live in poverty and receive little education, and an aging population needs more and more health care. There is widespread corruption in government at local, regional, and national levels, and industrial development has created dangerously high levels of air pollution. The government is putting its energy into solving these economic and social problems, rather than on political reform. The National People's Congress of China meets only once a year and has very few powers. It merely approves the decisions of the Communist Party.

This is a street protest by the Democratic Party of China. But it is being held in New York City, not in China. A democratic protest like this would not be allowed by China's ruling Communist Party.

声援
高智晟

中國民主黨全國委員會
DEMOCRATIC PARTY OF CHINA

UNDERSTANDING BETTER

WEALTH AND POLITICS

China's rapid economic growth has greatly increased the wealth of the millions of people who have moved from rural areas to the cities to work in factories. They have money to spend on goods and services. Car sales, for example, have more than doubled in just five years. Do you think that people with more financial independence are likely to want more political opportunities, too? Will they feel they deserve to have more of a say in how their country is run?

BARRIERS TO CHANGE

In 2013, new leaders of the Communist Party took office, unelected by the people. They continued the country's long history of authoritarian rule. However, with a population already exceeding 1.3 billion, a change to democracy would be a challenge for China. Could a parliament effectively represent this number of people? Would political change continue to support the country's recent economic progress? These are just some of the questions standing in the way of democratic reform.

Despite its communist government, China now has millions of citizens with money to spend on consumer goods. Large shopping malls like this one have opened in many of the country's cities.

What Have You Learned?

We have learned that democracy as a system of government has a very long history, but that the struggle to achieve it has been difficult. In some countries, democracy evolved over centuries. Other countries have tried to impose democracy quickly, in reaction to an oppressive government. Many countries are still without democracy, and the world's most widespread political system still faces many challenges in the modern world.

DEMOCRATIC PRINCIPLES

We have seen that national democracies are representative: The people elect politicians to represent them for a period of a few years. The executive branch makes policy decisions, the legislature debates those policies and makes laws, and the judiciary safeguards the use of the law equally, to all people. Citizens of a democracy can expect to enjoy freedom of expression and the protection of their human rights, including equality of opportunity regardless of gender, religion, or race. However, the people need to play an important role, too. Democracies only work effectively when both politicians and voters are actively involved in the decision-making process.

In South Africa, citizens waited in line to vote in a recent general election. Democracy is progressing in this country, which has the biggest economy of any in Africa.

THE FUTURE

Democracy is more fragile in some countries than others. In the West, for example, some people show signs of taking their democracy for granted, and losing interest in politics. In other countries, the people are fighting to gain the right to have a say in their government. However, most people agree that democracy is here to stay. Many people and organizations around the world are working to improve people's access to democracy, and to overcome the challenges it faces for the future.

In November 2012, NBC News transformed Rockefeller Center in New York City into Democracy Plaza, an interactive experience celebrating American democracy.

UNDERSTANDING BETTER

PERFECT POLITICS?

British Prime Minister Winston Churchill said in 1947, "Democracy is the worst form of government except all the others that have been tried from time to time." What he meant was that no form of government can be perfect. Democracy may be the most tried and tested political system, but will it stand up to the test of time? How well do you think democracies perform in protecting the rights of citizens and in giving them effective, stable government?

GLOSSARY

abolition to get rid of something, to make it illegal

absolute rule to rule without any challenge to one's authority

authoritarian a form of rule in which the opinion of others is not considered

barons men who held a lot of land during the medieval period

cabinet the meeting of members of the executive branch, or ministers

censoring controlling the information that people in a country receive

civil rights a movement that fought for equality for black people in the United States in the 1960s

coalition the joining of two or more political parties in order to rule

colonies countries that are ruled by another country, as part of an empire

communism a system of government where the state controls all wealth and property

constitution a set of rules and principles that lays out how a nation should be governed

dictatorship government by a leader who rules with absolute power

direct democracy when all the people make everyday decisions of government

discrimination excluding someone because of his or her gender, race, age, or religious beliefs

elite a group of people with privileges not available to everyone

executive branch the branch of government that creates policy and carries it out

fascism a political movement in favor of dictatorial, repressive government

federation a group of organizations or countries that join to enforce power or order

franchise the right to vote

hierarchical organized by rank, with the most powerful at the top

human rights rights that every human being has, regardless of where they live

judiciary the branch of government consisting of the judges and courts of law

jury a group of ordinary citizens called upon in a court of law to decide whether the tried person is guilty or innocent

legislature the branch of government that debates policy and makes laws

minister a person who is elected to help govern a country

monarchy rule by a king or queen, who usually inherits their role

nobility the upper classes in a monarchy

oppressive controlling with force

political party a group of people with similar ideas about how a country should be run

radicals people with extreme beliefs

referendum a vote open to all citizens on an issue of national importance

reform political or social change

representative democracy when the people elect politicians to represent them in government

republic a democracy where the head of state is also elected, rather than a hereditary monarch

revolution a violent upheaval to overthrow a ruler or bring radical change

socialism a political system where wealth is shared equally between the people

sovereignty supreme authority over a country

Soviet Union a union of communist countries in Eastern Europe, led by Russia, which lasted until 1991

suffrage the right to vote. Universal suffrage is the right of all adults to vote.

FOR MORE INFORMATION

BOOKS

Friedman, Mark. *The Democratic Process*.
Chicago, IL: Children's Press, 2012.

Leavitt, Amie Jane. *Who Really Created Democracy?*
North Mankato, MN: Capstone Press, 2011.

Ling, Bettina. *Aung San Suu Kyi: Standing Up for
Democracy in Burma*. New York, NY: The Feminist Press at CUNY, 1998.

WEBSITES

Find out more about the government of the United States at:
kids.usa.gov/government/index.shtml

Discover more about democracy at:
pbskids.org/democracy

Learn more about the history of democracy at:
ducksters.com/history/us_government.php

Find out about human rights at:
**humanrightseducation.info/images/stories/
pdf/HRD_simple_en.pdf**

Discover more about the British parliament system at:
parliament.uk/education/online-resources/parliament-explained

Publisher's note to educators and parents: Our editors have carefully reviewed these websites to ensure that they are suitable for students. Many websites change frequently, however, and we cannot guarantee that a site's future contents will continue to meet our high standards of quality and educational value. Be advised that students should be closely supervised whenever they access the Internet.

INDEX